How

Do You

Relate?

How Do You Relate?

by

Eloise Windahl-Deihl

Bless you
Eloise

LifeRich
PUBLISHING

LifeRich Publishing is a registered trademark of
The Reader's Digest Association, Inc.

LifeRich Publishing books may be ordered through booksellers or by contacting:

LifeRich Publishing
1663 Liberty Drive
Bloomington, IN 47403
www.liferichpublishing.com
1 (888) 238-8637

Because of the dynamic nature of the Internet, any web addresses or links contained in this book may have changed since publication and may no longer be valid. The views expressed in this work are solely those of the author and do not necessarily reflect the views of the publisher, and the publisher hereby disclaims any responsibility for them.

Any people depicted in stock imagery provided by Thinkstock are models, and such images are being used for illustrative purposes only. Certain stock imagery © Thinkstock.

ISBN: 978-1-4897-0220-3 (sc)
ISBN: 978-1-4897-0219-7 (e)

Library of Congress Control Number: 2014912044

Printed in the United States of America.

LifeRich Publishing rev. date: 08/07/2014

To my late husband, Don Deihl, for the many years of marriage, six children, and his hard work, love, and support.

To Pastor Ron Bakken and Faith Hope and Love Church for twenty-five years of great teaching, preaching, and Scripture that has greatly strengthened my "faith walk" and love of the Lord Jesus Christ.

Last but not least to my daughter Cherie Bratcher for her hours of helping type my manuscript and setting up a website. I am grateful for her advice in getting my book published, as she has recently published her own book, *Twin Identity*. Thank you very much!

Contents

Acknowledgments

Thank you to my six children, Paul, Jeff, Brian, Pam, Lorise, and Cherie—all "good Deihls" from whom I learned most of what I know about parenting. I would also like to thank my sisters, June, Dolores, and Phyllis, and brother, Norlan, from whom I learned about siblings.

My love and thanks to all of you!

Introduction

This may not lead you into a whole new world of thought, because the principles are timeless. However, relating them to the ages, stages, and many difficulties of life and finding solutions in God's Word will truly help you to find the best possible ways to relate on this earthly journey.

1
Adolescence

Life—what a fascinating journey. Isn't it amazing that no two human beings other than identical twins have ever been born exactly alike? Even they have different lives and experiences as they grow. Only our unspeakably awesome God accomplished that.

As we grow and then age, we all fulfill many different roles in life. One would think infancy would be the easiest, most carefree time in any human's life, right? Yet, for most people, we cry and shed more tears at this time than at any other period of our lives. Perhaps because it's the only language babies possess. Yet they express themselves quite well, don't they? Being the mother of first three sons and then three daughters, I know whereof I speak! Also, I was the fourth girl in a row in a family of five children. Three and a half years after me, they finally got their son. They were jubilant, I'm sure. To that I can relate, having had three sons first and then hoping for a girl. Our first roles in life are as babies and then as

1

children. We don't remember much about babyhood, but we can recall many things from our childhood.

Having raised six children, I can say they were and are all quite different. Our first roles in life are as children, and each of us has a different story to tell. We first learn to relate to Mommy, Daddy, sisters, and brothers, and that is the basis of forming our personalities and how we relate to others in our lives. The possibilities are endless. Each family member plays a part in shaping our personalities for good, bad, or indifferent—or a little of each. If we are children with few or many siblings, we know we relate a bit differently to each one of them. Why is that? Well, each one had a different temperament and personality, just like people outside the family, and we are more attracted to or repelled by different personalities and temperaments. We like some more and others less. It is a fact of life. As babies and children we pretty much act on feelings and cry or fuss to get our needs met or what we want. But when we are older, we are to leave childish things, as the Bible teaches us. So ideally what needs to happen to change that? The Bible clearly commands parents, "Train up a child in the way he or she should go and when they are old they will not depart from it" (Prov. 22:6).

What does that mean? That is huge and really places the ball squarely in the parent's court. You now have the responsibility and privilege, with God's help, of becoming a parent who will lead, guide, shape, and encourage that little person into becoming first and foremost one who will love and follow the Lord with all of his or her heart! How could you ask for anything more? If you do this, the child will much more readily accept all the other teachings that go into a truly noble character and person.

How does a parent do that? Well, through lots prayer and a lot of help from the Lord. Parents also need love and determination to live that kind of life themselves, which would be a great example. That will go a long way in helping your child to bring delight to you and the Lord. The Bible says you must use "the seat of learning" when necessary. Now there are no guarantees, as God gave us free will, and every human has his or her flesh, the world, and the Devil to deal with. But we have the assurance that if we do our part, our children will return to what they were thoroughly taught—that is, Jesus, the Bible, Sunday school and church, love, and godly living.

So as children our first relationships are with parents, and then with God, and then we relate to a brother or sister or some of each. The relationship also depends on whether you are the younger or older brother or sister. I was the fourth girl, and the sister next to me was seven and a half years older. By the time I was two, she was nine and a half, and so the competitive factor didn't exist for us in my growing-up years. Hers was more of a nurturing and teaching role since I was her little sister. I looked up to her as my big sister. That isn't always the case when brothers and sisters are closer in age. The competitive factor is so often present in those relationships.

Just a footnote here—science and biology classes were always the most fascinating to me. One year for Christmas I asked my parents for a chemistry set. To their chagrin, I sometimes smelled up the restaurant where we lived, and my parents would smell sulfur and other strange concoctions. In my senior year I took a psychology course, and the thick book we were issued fascinated me! I read it every chance I got—both in school and at home—as though it were a novel. So it didn't take me long to finish it even before we got far into studying it. Relationships have always fascinated me, and all my life I have read those types of articles. Though I am not licensed in that field, as I am in the cosmetology and beauty field, I claim the "qualifications" of being an up-close-and-personal observer, and, yes, a chair-side "psychologist" to some of my beauty clients.

As children, we learn to take in vast amounts of information day by day and year by year since we come into this world with instincts but knowing almost zero. Since all three of my sisters are years older than I, as the little sister I never felt the competitiveness that is so common among siblings who are close in age. That would have been more likely with the third sister. So frequently children vie for more of their parents' love and attention, privileges, and clothing. Everything has to be "fair" in a child's mind regardless of age. So how, as a younger or older sibling, can you relate?

If you are a young person at home or are an older sibling, how is your relationship right now? Are there rough spots? Do you wish things were better? Are they recent difficult issues or long-standing? Obviously there are hurt and painful feelings and memories, and in all likelihood you believe the sister or brother is mostly to blame. Possibly he or she is, or maybe not, but deep down you wish there was some way to have a more friendly, even loving, relationship with that sibling. Now when

I was three years and four months old, we got a baby brother, and we were all ecstatic! What a novelty in a family of all girls! It was smooth for a long time until we got a little older. Then of course like all sisters and brothers we had our differences. Those were minor and soon gotten over. But one was deeper and longer lasting, so of course it was painful. During my recovery from open-heart surgery, my sisters and brother sent cards and flowers, and the healing began (pun intended). It took a while, but we now have a good relationship.

Prayer and forgiveness were involved on both sides I'm sure. Crises can have a way of solving and healing relationships, but letting things go they can grow and fester and possibly leave scars and is not good! Unfortunately that's the way division and separation can go on for years, sometimes indefinitely. What a shame of time lost time, painful thoughts, hurtful feelings of blame, and bitterness, possibly even impacting one's health and longevity. You may have memories of good times together and wish there was some way of getting those back!

First let's not pretend it's easy because there are perhaps strong feelings of hurt and blame to deal with. First examine and reexamine the situation and see if in all honesty you are 100 percent blameless in any part of it. This is a good starting place. Like a building needs a good foundation, you can move up from there. If you have sincerely prayed for guidance and feel you are not guilty, then there is the issue of forgiveness to deal with! Depending on the size of the situation, you will probably find it one of the most difficult things you have ever had to deal with! We have rehashed and replayed it so many times that our hearts, minds, and flesh rebel. We think we can't do it, but it's really that we won't do it! Perhaps that's the reason the Lord Jesus said we must forgive seventy times seven. As Corrie ten Boom said, like a ringing bell, the "bim bams" come back, and if she could and did forgive the man in the concentration camp who killed her father and her sister, then our issues may be pretty small in comparison.

Notes: How will you relate?

_____

_____

_____

_____

_____

_____

_____

2
Siblings

The next step is to consider your approach to your brother or sister. After you have prayed, by an act of your will say, "I forgive (then say their name), and you are forgiven!" Take a deep breath and pause a moment. You may or may not feel immediately that a weight has been lifted from your heart and shoulders, but you will soon feel a freeing in your spirit because you have been obedient. These bad feelings have controlled you for too long. When the Devil tries to bring these thoughts and feelings back to you, just say, "In the name of Jesus, just bug off!" They are forgiven! Then ask God to bless them and save them if they need salvation.

The next step in this restoration process is communicating with them. Sincerely state your feelings and desires to get together with them to discuss and smooth out some rough spots in your relationship. Have a kind, friendly tone of voice. Choose your words well, and set a time and place. Determine in your heart and attitude not to get angry all over again! Pray that you convey kindness and openness. State "I feel" or "I think" without being accusatory like, "You did this" or "You said that" in a mean tone of voice. You will probably receive what you give. Kindness usually begets kindness. Don't give up; you have made progress even if you have to start again!

The next role in a child's life is with caregivers and then as a student in school. The hope is that parents begin at an early age to first be exemplary role models in godliness, kindness to spouses, and family members and to be generous and have good manners and language. Sounds like a tall order, and we all fall short at times. But no one said parenting is easy! Only with God's help can we be such parents. But that is the best way to help a child grow and become a person who can relate well in all the roles in life he or she will fulfill.

Next children will be students. Oh the challenges they will face relating to all the teachers they will encounter in life! All of us have been there, done that! Most of us had teachers we really, really liked and others had varying degrees of connection, liking, and disliking.

You can prepare your child for that certainty, even your kindergartener. Speaking at your children's language level, before their first day, use a story about two kinds of kindergartners who had a firm teacher and how one of them reacted badly and was sassy and fussed a lot every day, so the teacher had to deal with the child, correcting and scolding. The other child listened quietly and politely, smiling if it was funny and not starting fights. The teacher treated that child so much more respectfully, and they had a nice, even fun time together. Now ask the child to tell the story back to you. Then ask which child he or she would like to be like. Then emphasize how much easier, nicer, and more fun school will be if you act like the nicer child!

As the days go, by ask your child how it's working. Maybe ask for an example. It's good reinforcement. Tell your child if he or she wants to be a really big boy or girl, to try to be nice to someone who seems to be in trouble all the time and help that person. If your child seems to be more like the troubled one, it will take more effort, but if you send your child off with a short prayer and a warm hug, it may bring changes. Have your child say the prayer with you. Assure your child that he or she is a special and loved child and it will help him or her to "relate better." Having the assurance and certainty of parents' love goes a long way in a child's progress and life. Children who feel unloved and neglected by parents are often the troubled and troubling students.

Notes: How will you relate?

_____

_____

_____

_____

_____

_____

_____

3
Employee

The next step in life's journey from student is usually to being an employee. Oh the variations one finds on that path, such as relations with your supervisor, your boss, and other employees. That path could be fraught with every conceivable roadblock to success. You may encounter personality types ranging from very good to bad to awful.

So how can you respond to all of the above? The single best thing you can do in the beginning is to be an interested listener and observer. What will this do for you? 1. People like good listeners. 2. You will learn what your job is about, what is expected of you, and something about your boss's personality type. These are powerful tools in your arsenal for success. Cultivate being a good listener, and then apply yourself diligently to your goals. With prayer and God's guidance, you will be a success.

There will be difficult circumstances and people along

the way. There almost always are. One frequent danger to be very aware of is competitive coworkers who are not above undermining you with half-truths and untruths to the boss. Don't allow that to go unaddressed! That was a huge mistake I made at one job. Coworkers were telling outright untruths to our supervisor, which she would write up and put in my file. She then came to me with warnings to change and stop doing what they said I had been doing. Well I was shocked to say the least! They both were doing very rule-breaking things against me to boost their daily sales goals. They had run to her and lied before, so if I complained, she wouldn't believe me. I had naively believed as adults we could straighten it out without running to the supervisor. Unfortunately they continued the deceit, and I lost my job!

Those things must be confronted and dealt with before it's too late. With the Lord's help, I found a better job, with better pay and a situation with good people. But the lesson I learned was I should have confronted the girls early, as soon as they clearly were breaking the rules and making me look bad. Even good, God-loving Christians should not allow themselves to be lied about. If you as an employee find yourself in a bad situation, be sure you are giving your best. Pray for guidance and then act. That's the best way to relate as an employee. God will either improve the situation or help you find a better one.

Notes: How will you relate?

_____

_____

_____

_____

_____

_____

_____

4
Dating/Marriage

The next step in one's life after being a student and employee is often dating and marriage. Dating can be filled with fun, joy, and complexities! What an interesting period in one's life. Today there is a whole different range of options that didn't exist when I was in that period of my life. It's almost mind boggling that there are numerous dating services to choose from and all the techy connections of Twitter, Facebook, and even dating pages in the newspapers. There is even speed dating, where you sit for a few minutes with someone, ask quick questions, and then move on to the next one. How strange is that? Yet in spite of all the help to find a good match and mate, the divorce rate is higher than it has ever been! Something is truly wrong somewhere.

First and foremost at every stage in life is having a personal relationship with God through Jesus Christ, who created us. So how do you relate? Have you taken the most-important step and made the most-important decision a human being will ever make in his or her lifetime? That is asking Jesus Christ to come into your life to forgive and cleanse you of all your sins, to believe he rose from the dead to become the Lord of your life. If you do this, you will become a child of God and inherit heaven and eternal life. There is nothing in this world that is of as great a value!

When it comes to finding and choosing a life partner you have the greatest guide that could exist. First and foremost you will only look for a date with a true God-loving believer. God's Word, the Bible, says, "Be not unequally yoked together with an unbeliever for what fellowship can a believer have with an unbeliever?" You would only be asking for trouble. So find a lively, worshipful, loving church, and you will find it's one of the very best places to find a date and mate. In this circumstance and place, God can lead and guide you. So prayerfully seek his help. When you do, you will have the assurance that this is the right partner for you. It beats every other method that is completely hollow.

Now you are a married husband or wife, so how do you relate best? If you are the husband, the Bible says a man should love his wife as deeply as God loves his church and gave his life for it. That is a lot of love! He is to love his wife as his own body and nurture and care for her. And he is to leave his father and mother. If you are the wife, you are to respect your husband and defer to him. You are to love and honor and care for him. If couples truly lived as they ought, there wouldn't be many divorces at all. First of all only date people of faith with whom you have interests in common and who you feel you might deeply love and God leads you to marry. If you want to truly relate as a spouse in a good, happy marriage, you cannot be selfish and want everything your way. There will need to be a lot of flexibility, compromise, and give and take. In disagreements, try hard to use civil tones, and leave out the sarcasm. Lighten things up with some humor; it can go a long way if appropriate. To love and serve God and each other is a sure recipe for a lasting, happy marriage. Being able to say I am sorry and I love you is huge!

Notes: How will you relate?

_____

_____

_____

_____

_____

_____

_____

5
Parenting

The next role in life you play is probably as a mom or dad. Oh the joys, sweat, and tears. We have covered some of the attributes of good parenting in the child's section, but there are many stages to being a parent! Tons of books and articles on parenting continue to be written. One of my reliable go-to helps was Dr. Spock's well-known book. But everything seems to change and needs updating. The one source that never changes or needs updating is the rock-solid word of God, so that and a current good baby and childcare book is what you need. One thing that has stayed the best advice is that breastfeeding is the most superior, *healthiest* way to feed your infant. That is what I did for about a year each for all six of our children. There also is no better way to bond mother and baby than that. If at all possible, do it at least for a while. It's the best, most natural way to relate as a mommy, and it has been found to give some long-term health benefits of immunity and various things. Oh yes, and also get a good thermometer.

The first child for most couples is the most challenging since it's all new and you're just learning. If you get to feeling stressed out, take several good, deep breaths and ask our heavenly Father for help and guidance. You will feel better! The basic needs of a baby aren't too complicated. They need to be fed, kept dry and not too warm, bathed, and cuddled. Establish routines, and don't pick them up at every little whimper. They learn quickly and can soon have you under their thumb. A little bit of discipline for yourself and them is definitely in order. If they are fussy, dry, and burped, allow them to cry awhile. Oh how fast they grow! Hopefully church and Sunday school is part of their entire growing-up life. Again the Bible says, "Train up a child in the way they should go and when they are old they will not depart from it" (Proverbs 22:6). Give them an easy-to-read Bible at an early age and read to them fascinating Bible stories from children's books, and it will seem a natural part of their lives. Since there is so much junk all around, good choices and early training are essential in molding good character, and parents must model love and kindness!

Early on give them small chores to do consistently and help around the home and with pets if you have them. This way they won't grow up expecting to be served and waited on hand and foot. You want them to have a good work ethic. Above all, teach them to love God and people and to have a healthy love and respect for themselves also. The years pass, kids are away at school, and you now have an empty nest. It takes a bit of getting used to. But with the ubiquitous iPads and cell phones, they don't seem far away. Yet you are no longer on diaper duty, and you do have a little more time for you and your spouse.

Now how will you relate? There was a discussion this morning on a TV program about how to break a habit and start a new one. Three of the elements in a habit are: 1. cue, 2. the doing or performance of it, and 3. the pleasure or reward of doing it. Cue is the time of morning, noon, afternoon, and evening you're prompted to do certain things, and they can become deeply ingrained habits for good, bad, or indifferent. Say you want to break one of those and replace it with something better, healthier, or more purposeful and meaningful. It is a good plan to use that very same pattern. Set the time of day or evening for the same time as the habit you want to break (your cue), and then perform the new action. After or during the action, experience a pleasure or at the completion of it, have a little reward. Keep doing this, and a new good habit can be established.

So what habits would you like to change? Now is a really good time to give more attention to your spouse and yourself. It is an opportunity to put a little spice and life back into your marriage! By now you know each other's interest, likes and dislikes, joys and sorrows. So why not plan a little getaway to some place new and different, even if it can only be a brief one, like a long weekend to someplace you would both enjoy? Put some real energy into being considerate and sweet to each other and it can really ignite a new dimension into your marriage. Try it! Life is too short to just exist and accommodate in a marriage. Now practice it every day. It's so much easier when it's just the two of you. When an anniversary is approaching, why not plan a second honeymoon? It can work wonders if you want it to! So, how will you relate?

Eloise Windahl-Deihl

Notes: How will you relate?

_____

_____

_____

_____

_____

_____

_____

6
In-Laws

The next person you will become is probably an in-law (should be different than an outlaw). When your adult child becomes engaged, you will have some practice time. Your feelings about your son or daughter's choice may range from strong disapproval, tolerance, kind of like, or oh, I just love him or her. Wow, that last one sure makes it easy! So how do you use your practice time? First listen, then observe. Don't make any snap judgments! If your son or daughter is a committed Christian, that's the first thing you will want to know. If that potential spouse is not, that would be a primary reason to have a serious cautionary conversation with your son or daughter. Remind your child that his or her fiancé must be given an opportunity to sincerely commit his or her life to the Lord and follow Him before the marriage or break it off.

That's hard but there's no guarantee the spouse will do so after the marriage, and the Bible is very clear where it says, "Be not unequally yoked together with an unbeliever for harmony is at odds and there is not fellowship together with God" (2 Corinthians 6:14). It causes many problems in the marriage and in child rearing. If you are wise and obedient to the Lord, don't do it. He will help you find a believing, faithful, God-loving mate if you are asking and trusting Him to do so. Then you can really relate!

Notes: How will you relate?

_____

_____

_____

_____

_____

_____

_____

7
Grandparent

The next role you are likely to find yourself in is grandparent. Oh, how many people seem to delight in their grandchildren! I think the reason is because it's kind of like a second chance. You've got experience and wisdom and not the responsibilities. Now it's time to have fun with your grandkids. A note of caution: have fun but don't undermine the parents' rules and training that are good and godly! Spoiling children can be just that. Love and generosity are good so long as it's not way overdone. Teach respect and good manners and how to pray from the time they are very small. Then those little ones can grow into the kind of adults you can always love, be proud of, and brag (a little bit) about. That's how you as a grandparent can relate.

The next role in life is likely as a retired and elderly person. So many paths and choices await you! They are endless, especially if, like me, your spouse has moved to heaven. If your health is still quite good, take steps to keep and improve it. After having and helping to raise and educate six children, as I mentioned earlier, I have experienced some major health challenges—first glaucoma, then diabetes, and then a heart attack that required open-heart bypass surgery. But my claim is that I am healed of the Lord, and I truly enjoy an amazing life. I have helped plan and been part of many weddings, along with my good husband, Don, who gave away three daughters. We enjoyed becoming grandparents and have nine of them, and Don got to see a picture of our first great-grandson before he moved to heaven.

To celebrate our twenty-fifth wedding anniversary, we took a twenty-one-day tour in Europe. It was an amazing trip through eleven countries. Don had been in Paris, Germany, and Amsterdam during his military service. This trip we took just whetted my appetite for travel. My working career, besides raising sons and daughters, was cosmetology while we lived in California and had five children there. We moved back to Minnesota, where I had a beauty salon in our new home in Fosston and one more daughter to even things up. Twelve years later we moved to the Moorhead, Minnesota, area, which borders Fargo, North Dakota. There I worked in cosmetics and switched to insurance and retired at age sixty-seven.

Those were also the years when I went through those major health challenges. But the Lord brought me through them all and restored my usual good health and energy. I sort of doubled down, eating healthy, taking a whole spectrum of good nutrients, and quitting some prescriptions. Condition-specific nutrients took their place! Make sure to talk to your doctor before doing so. I do aerobics and lift weights in front of the TV as I watch good Christian programs in the morning, four days a week. One day a week I vacuum my church for about an hour and a half. Those are some of the ways I relate to being elderly!

I do love to travel so the many different routes we took going back to visit family in Minnesota. When we lived in California, traveling by both cars and trains was an adventure even with our kids! In 1988 my sister Phyllis and I went on a bus trip for Walk for Life in Washington, DC. Wow, what an interesting trip in our capitol! People from over a hundred other countries marched for the pro-life cause!

God is so good; I've gone on three more tours to Europe and one through Spain, where I saw our daughter who was stationed outside Madrid at Terhone Air Base. We got to visit in Madrid, and then the tour I was with went on into Africa. What a fascinating trip! The more you see, the more you want to see and experience. At least that's been my experience.

I have been blessed to have been prompted by the Lord to go on three different mission trips. What a privilege to help spread the gospel! The first was to Monterrey, Mexico, the second to Acapulco, and the last one to Beijing, China. Each one was so different, but many souls were reached for the Lord. An added bonus was a walk on the Great Wall and also a wild rickshaw ride with Pastor Ron, wow! I have taken four amazing tours to thirteen countries (one was Norway) in Europe. I have been there, done that.

When I looked at a map, I counted thirty-eight states

I have been through. Oh, and I finally took my first cruise with my daughter about three years ago. We visited the Caribbean Islands and Jamaica. It was delightful, and the food was amazing. I never thought I would enjoy a cruise so much. My sister Phyllis and I enjoyed a trip to Branson, Missouri, together, and we had a delightful time and fellowship as she truly loves and serves the Lord. My yearly trips to Arizona ended when my dear sister Dolores moved to heaven. Oh how I miss her! Well since one of my daughters and family lives in San Antonio and another daughter in Florida, I have two great places to visit and take a month out of our Minnesota winter. How about that?

The reason I gave you my travel log is proof of what God can and will do if you have a little willingness and obedience to love and serve Him. He can restore health and provide for all your needs. He is now helping and using this elderly dame to speak and sing for Christian women's clubs. I have been in four states and am still traveling. I just celebrated another birthday on May 8, followed by Mother's Day. I'm not sure "celebrate" is the right word, unlike when I was very young, but my children make it a lovely time! Oh yes, age is just a number, and mine is unlisted!

Notes: How will you relate?

_____

_____

_____

_____

_____

_____

_____

8
Old Age

The next step in life is accepting and adapting to old age. More and more people are living long lives. I have a dear sister who at ninety-four still lives alone in a split-level house. She passed her driving test and drives to church and shopping. Another sister and husband are eighty-seven and eighty-nine! They still drive and travel and grow a big garden. She cans lovely food, and he still hunts and fishes with their kids and grandkids. Granted, my sisters are a good bit older than I, but I have a lot to live up to.

So what should we all do? Well, your self-talk is an excellent place to start. We need to make positive faith statements, not claiming sickness and disease. What you say is what you get! If you currently have a condition, say, "I believe the Lord will heal me and restore my health." Of course doctors have their place. The Bible is full of promises of healing if you by faith claim it. Look in a Bible concordance for a long list of healing Scripture. The Lord wants you well! He went about doing good and healing all of people's diseases. It's never the Lord who puts sickness and disease on his children. It is Satan who goes about as a roaring lion seeking whom he may destroy and devour.

The best statement and self-talk you can make is, "I am the healed of the Lord. By his stripes I was healed." Check out Psalm 10:3, Isaiah 5:3–5, 3 John 2, and so many others. The Lord wants his children to walk in divine health even more than we want our children to be healthy. So if you have an illness or a condition that needs healing, ask a pastor in a church who practices laying hands on the sick or deacons and elders who do that to pray for healing. After hands-on prayer, receive it in faith. Thank and praise the Lord for it. Continue to say, "I am the healed of the Lord!"

Words are powerful, and as you continue in every area of your life to speak positively and place your faith in Jesus Christ, you will be amazed at the changes that will begin to happen to you. There is huge truth in a little saying from long ago that goes like this: "You got to accentuate the positive, eliminate the negative." By stating any or many negative things in or about your life, it opens the door for the Evil One to work in and make sure they become reality. The Bible does say out of the mouth come the issues of life and death. What we say can and will influence a great deal of what happens in our lives. So speak what and who you are in Christ and "all the things he provides for his children. Remember God's word says "Every promise in the book is mine".

That reminds me that I have been speaking and singing at a Christian coffeehouse and ministry in Fargo several times a year for many years. I very often use a scriptural promise book and strongly suggest every

Christian have at least one. They are arranged topically in alphabetical order, and you can find just the Scripture promises you need for any situation in seconds. They are comforting and reassuring for you in times of need as well as a great tool in helping others with specific problems. Yes a concordance is good, but a promise book is so good, so fast when you need help. My concordance has many paragraphs about the function of angels in both the Old Testament and new, and it is very interesting how they are to minister to the righteous. Rest assured you have a guardian angel. It says in Psalm 91:11, "For he shall give his angels charge over thee to keep thee in all thy way." Isn't that a wonderful, comforting promise? It's true we don't pray to angels, but we can cry out to the Lord for help and know they are on duty!

So in old age how do you relate? Years ago while I was living in Fosston, Minnesota, and had a beauty salon with four of the six children still in our home with one married and one in college, I wanted a Baldwin piano. I also wanted a Christmas trip back to California to visit relatives and friends where we had lived for twelve years and where five of our six children were born in Holtville, California. Since my salon was closed on Sunday and Monday, I decided to work three nights a week, the 11:00 p.m. to 7:00 a.m. shift at a nursing home within walking distance. After all, my husband, Don, always worked long and hard to provide a nice home for his family. His sister Rachael and family and his brother Dave and family lived in California, so it would be a great trip to see them and our friends. I took the nursing home job to make those two goals a reality.

There were about twenty-eight men and women in

this nursing home, and my job was to dust the common area, do laundry, bake cookies, and then help dress people and make beds in the morning. That was my up close and personal contact with old people, as well as several in the beauty salon. Oh my, how different they all were! Even way back then not every old person fit the stereotype. Usually then as now it is people who have a close personal relationship with the Lord who have the healthier, happier outlook on life. At the nursing home I encountered all types of people: the chronic complainers, the stoics, the optimists, and a few happy people. Of course health and circumstances factor into it, but the happier people's lives hadn't been a bed of roses either. A strong faith in God makes a difference! When it comes to old age, how do you relate? So much of it is choice! I can't emphasize that enough! Your self-talk as well as having a close speaking relationship with the Lord are both important.

Notes: How will you relate?

_____

_____

_____

_____

_____

_____

_____

9
Health

How are your eating habits? Are they healthy, or are they harming your chances of living a long, healthy life? Do you regularly walk and get good exercise? How about a daily serving of God's Word? That alone can make a huge difference in your outlook and expectations.

We've all heard the accounts of many people who have briefly died and found themselves in heaven. They told us how unbelievably beautiful the setting and music were and what it was like to meet loved ones who were already there. A few have told about finding themselves in hell and how unspeakably horrific the torment and suffering and pain all around is. How thankful they were to be brought back to life and have a second chance! So when it comes to eternity, how do you relate? These numerous firsthand accounts certainly put the lie to atheists' and doubters' assertions that there is no eternity in heaven or hell.

The Bible is absolute truth. That's why Jesus paid the

price for us; he got a look at the horrors of hell and then rose from death on the third day. Now we all can choose the gift of eternal life in paradise with him and all of our loved ones who had a personal relationship with Christ the Savior. His arms are open wide to any and all who come to him and ask forgiveness of all their sins and invite him into their hearts and lives to be their Lord. Treat yourself to the joy of a good Bible, and find a happy and welcoming church family! Amen, now you truly relate.

Notes: How will you relate?

_____

_____

_____

_____

_____

_____

_____

10
Widow

Oh widowhood—the time in life of another major change! There is grief, loss, trauma, funeral arrangements, financial concerns, living arrangements, health, living alone, and fear of the unknown. It's considerably more complex than the empty-nest syndrome. You can feel overwhelmed! The saving grace is, as mine was, your children's help. I can't imagine how hard it would have been without them. So how will you relate?

I was in bed and got the call at six in the morning from the VA hospital that Don had passed. "Please come up as soon as you can." That was the first thing I had to do and then begin the arrangements and decide what funeral home to take him to. Then I had myriad calls to make, especially one to the Lord for help and guidance with all the decisions to be made. My daughter who lives in Minnesota came to help with the entire decision making. It's first things first and one step at a time. From the obituary to casket choice, pallbearers, bulletin, flowers, the funeral, Scripture, music, burial arrangements, the clothes he would wear, church kitchen arrangements, and the list goes on and on. Thankfully I received the help I needed. They all came through—my kids, my pastors, the funeral home, and even a military salute. So God was my ever-present help in time of trouble. That's just the first step, the beginning of widowhood, all the paperwork and legal ends to tie up, banks, and wills, and so on. Cleaning out closets can be hard too.

When you know your spouse loved and served the Lord, you are aware that he or she is in Paradise with the Lord and our loved ones who went before and are more alive and in beautiful surroundings words can't describe. Remember Jesus said to the thief on the cross who repented, "Today you will be with me in paradise" (Luke 23:43). How wonderful to keep that close to your heart. If you are a child of God, you will join them all there. Joy unspeakable and full of glory! In the meantime you will have many adjustments to make and perhaps large ones like me, selling your home (a large four bedroom), emptying rooms, selling lots of stuff, trying to be fair to six kids, and then looking, finding, and buying a new place to live. With the Lord's help, I made it, and you can too!

So how do you relate to widowhood? Bottom line: put your faith and trust daily in the Lord's help through prayer and then positive self-talk. Use your promise book of Scripture for specific needs of promises to stand on, such as finances, good health, or a home. You will find what you need. He will be with you daily and comfort, teach, and lead you as you lean and trust in him. Again, being in a good, alive, friendly church with a terrific pastor and loving people who become your extended family is priceless! You won't find a better way as a widow to relate!

Notes: How will you relate?

_____

_____

_____

_____

_____

_____

_____

11
Change in Family Dynamics

How Do You Relate? This book deals with all the different roles in life we may fulfill. Every day we relate to different circumstances. I indicated in a previous chapter that I fulfilled all the roles that have brought me up to the present as a grandmother, retiree, and widow. Yes, it's true I have lived for several decades. I have been blessed to have a husband for many years who helped raise three sons and three daughters in that order. I now have almost six years of practice of being a widow. So how do I relate?

Change is the operative word. When I was twelve, my parents left the farm and went into operating a restaurant in a small town called Viking, Minnesota. That was a huge change for them and for my little brother, Norlan, and me. We adapted fairly quickly to the availability of candy, pop, and ice cream. But adapting to being alone after so many years of family and a husband is different and not easy. It comes with lots of decisions and responsibility. Certainly the presence of children and grandchildren help make a very big difference.

Change is inevitable in life. Had we not had the Lord's constant presence help and guidance through those years of Don's illness, life would have been a lot more unbearable. "He giveth more grace when the burdens grow greater, He sendeth more strength when labor increase." I have sung that song, and that's how we related to God and each other. There is no better way! We see changes come at every age and stage of life. Some changes come easy and some not so easy. The changes in the world and especially in our country that I have seen in my lifetime are mind numbing!

As a little girl on the farm, there of course was hard work. We all had our chores. There was even a war going on. Life was certainly not a bed of roses. Yet there was a strong feeling of patriotism and "we're all in this together." Life was simpler, not the frantic pace so many are caught up in. Some of the grievous changes I have seen over the years are morality on a continuous downward slide! The list is so long.

If you're middle aged or older you know all the societal changes. Profanity is on the streets, in television, and even said among children. Sexual morals have disappeared. Very young teens not using contraceptives, and huge numbers of out-of-wedlock children are the result. Rudeness can be seen and heard in almost any situation—in the workplace, in homes, at large gatherings, in stores, and on highways. Bad manners are witnessed often. It seems there is a lack of teaching good manners or common courtesy in the home too often and in our schools too. It's really refreshing when you encounter young people with good manners and even adults for that matter. It appears there's a coarsening of our sensibilities and consciences toward life as we've had forty years and fifty-five million aborted babies in the United States. Now we are making it legal for same-sex couples to marry even though the Bible strongly condemns it in both the Old Testament and the New! It definitely bears out what the Bible describes about the last days (Mark 4:19).

So how do we of the older generation cope and relate in a changing world? Well if we are a child of God, we will love God with all our hearts and our neighbors as ourselves, as the Bible instructs. We don't have permission to take on the world's lifestyle. In fact, we are to grow in grace and holiness. How? Being in the word and prayer and hearing the Word in a lively, welcoming, Spirit-led church! That is absolutely a huge part of my life. My church is my extended family, so that is how I choose to relate and live a happy, fulfilling life in a constantly changing world. Wherever you go, wherever you look people are attached to their new techy gadgets. It's even more perilous to drive the highways these days! I know our guardian angels have to be on overtime. I thank God!

I believe people of any age need to do the common-sense things to promote good health even into older age so you can continue to do the things you enjoy. Not long ago I had to smile when my daughter said, "The older we get, I think we become our mothers." There's some truth to that. I continue to exercise daily, my daughters exercise, and my mom exercised while watching Jack LaLanne, and she lived to be over eighty-six. There is benefit in that and in eating plenty of healthy fruits and veggies and taking some good multivitamins. As I mentioned earlier, I have a sister who is ninety-five and one who is eighty-seven. They both still have their driver's licenses and live in their split-level homes! I have a lot to live up to.

The important thing for us seniors is to stay involved and active as much as we can. Even though both of my sisters are years older than I, they both had large families; they have remained very involved with them, their churches, and their friends and neighbors. That may very well be part of their longevity!

Retirement is looked forward to by some and dreaded by others. Yes health and finances play a large part to how we relate to that stage of our lives. But we probably all know people who have not had much of either one and have continued to live full, satisfying lives into old age. How do you suppose they have done that? Let's count the ways.

First is attitude and expectations about retirement and getting older. If you've accepted it as all downward the rest of your days, it probably will be. If you consider these golden years with many opportunities, then most likely they will be. There is a lot of truth in the saying, "Life is what you make it!" There is a newer one that seniors like to quote that says, "Seventy is the new sixty." Attitude is so important; if you need an adjustment, take it to the Lord in prayer!

Planning and goals are important and not just letting things happen. This is finally your time in life to pursue dreams and hobbies, develop some hidden talents, and travel. Whatever trips your trigger, if it's wholesome and legal, go for it! I've had piano lessons, but I had a yen to learn guitar, so I bought one and have taken a few lessons. I practice it several times a week and am making some progress. I may take a few more lessons down the road.

I do practice what I preach by exercising, taking great vitamins, and keeping my weight down. Considering that about twelve years ago I was diagnosed with glaucoma, then diabetes, and then had a heart attack and open-heart bypass surgery, I've come a long way! Now my confession is, "I am the healed of the Lord!" I live a busy, active life. I continue to travel to speak and sing for Christian women's clubs since 2006 and have been in four states speaking. I recount the bumps in the road to show that my life of raising a large family of six kids and a variety of health challenges haven't kept me from traveling and doing the things I want to do and the things the Lord wants me to do, like the mission trips to Mexico and China and also speaking as long as the Lord directs me to. Oh, I guess I haven't mentioned that I am a twenty-five-year member of Toastmasters club and continue to hone my speaking and writing skills. It's another opportunity to stay involved and relate to people and help new members to achieve their goals. I am thoroughly enjoying the journey!

When I moved from Dilworth and a four-level, four-bedroom house, I had prayed for a nice place close to my church, and yes, a fireplace would be nice. One Sunday pastor Connie said, "Eloise, you should go and look at two condos that are for sale. It's just a stone's throw from the church. You really should go!" So my realtor and I went, and then I took my daughter and family to look at it again.

I bought a nice home up on sixth floor. It's a corner unit one with a lovely view and fireplace. It's only two minutes from church, and I drive under three bridges, saving me waiting on endless trains daily! Oh God is so amazingly great! I really love it here. It is easy to be involved in the many weekly activities here in my church. It's how I relate to the Lord and my church family. You can also find joy and relationships and help and companionships in a good church. If that doesn't describe your church, really pray about it, and ask the Lord to lead you to an alive, Spirit-filled church. It may take visiting a few churches, but you'll know in your spirit when you've found the right one. In your older years, this can be the most fulfilling and rewarding aspect of your life!

You know it's possible to grow old and sweet instead of old and crotchety I believe my two older sisters are sweeter than ever. My older sister Dolores was eighty-six when she went to heaven and was a real sweetheart of a gal. How do we do that? Well first and foremost is to know, love, and trust the Lord! As you walk with him for many years and see his great love for you and count your blessings daily, he can put love in your heart for people as you progress in the word and prayer. It is a joy to encounter elderly Christians who are genuinely content and happy and interested in and like people. What a lovely way to relate! Even when life and health aren't a bed of roses, God is the active force in their lives.

Notes: How will you relate?

_____

_____

_____

_____

_____

_____

_____

12
Maintaining Relationships

For us elderly folks, maintaining good strong, vibrant family relationships are hugely important. It adds so much to our later years. If some of yours need improvement, be courageous and make the effort. You might say, "This relationship is so bad. We haven't spoken for quite some time. What can I do?" Well think, do you really want to go to your grave carrying hatred, bitterness, and non-forgiveness toward any human being, especially a family member or relative? Doesn't the Lord's Prayer require us to forgive others if we expect to be forgiven? Your first step might be a well-thought-out letter. Use a little self-deprecation or a little humor, and state honestly how you feel. You may want to forgive and forget and put it all behind you. Ask if they are willing to do that and make a new start. Letters are great because they are real, in the person's hand, and can be read over and over. Or put your thoughts on paper and in a kind tone of voice call that person. If the person refuses (most won't) then you have set yourself free and done what you needed to do. He or she may come around. Now you can enjoy sweeter sleep. What a godly way to relate.

Some of you may be carrying around guilt of having taken something from somewhere or someone that didn't belong to you. It's an ongoing sore that never heals. Don't go to the grave with that on your conscience! Whether it's an object or something like an idea, a job, a friend, whatever it was, no matter how recent or long ago, it's never too late! Do whatever self-talk it takes to do the right thing! Go to the place or person, and admit and apologize sincerely and offer restitution where necessary or possible. It takes courage to do it, but it's oh so freeing, like a weight has been lifted off your shoulders. How nice to relate to your clear conscience.

In this country there are vast numbers of divorced couples, even among Christians. In far too many cases their remains rancor, bitterness, hurt feelings, even hatred. It can involve many people on both sides. Children are usually the most damaged. If you are one of these, truly it doesn't have to remain that way. No it isn't simple, and human relations seldom are. There are powerful emotions often involved, custody battles, and financial considerations. There is the blame game, infidelity, relatives' involvement, etc. In spite of all this, change is possible. So where do you begin? Only with a strong desire can things change. As a believer, make a sincere prayer for guidance, and you will receive it. I have seen it up close and personal the divorce of several people I care about and love. Each one had similarities and differences, and each one was painful and touched the lives of many people. If you are contemplating divorce, unless there is infidelity or violence involved, pray long and hard to bring about change. Seek pastoral counseling to heal and save your marriage.

If you are in the process of divorce, seek God's will and turn around if possible. If it's not, what can you do to lessen the trauma and pain? Again pray for guidance for strength and unselfishness. You want to cause the least amount of pain and upheaval to your children. Pray that you will not be consumed with revenge and greed. Do you really want your family and children to see you in that way?

Do not bad mouth to destroy the love and respect your children have for the other parent. That reeks of hate and is completely ungodly! Would you want that to be done to you? Instead keep the best interests of your children at heart in every respect as it impacts the rest of their lives. Treat your spouse with respect (with God's help) during these proceedings. The Bible clearly says that God hates divorce. You should proceed and act with dignity and fairness. No matter what, you need to preserve a civil relationship with your spouse if you have children at home that you will be sharing. Forgiving and amicable is better by far! Nursing bitterness leaves scars and sours your outlook. God can sustain you through this ordeal if you walk and lean on Him daily. Your Bible and a good scriptural promise book can be your lifeline back to a happy, healthy, fulfilling life. If you can mend and restore a relationship with the in-laws, by all means do it! It's important for your children. It can also be good for your self-esteem. Forgiveness can be so cleansing and freeing. That's how you can relate after a breakup.

The pattern of mending all relationships can start with some genuine soul-searching. The ones of long standing often seem the most difficult to repair and heal. You have replayed them over and over a hundred times in your mind, and they have become so deeply ingrained, you think you can never get rid of them. Been there, done that! Yes even as a committed, God-loving Christian, I've been there, and perhaps that makes the guilt even worse. I knew the requirement that I must forgive. But the raw pain of knowing I had been deeply, unfairly wronged kept hammering at me like a battering ram! And oh boy did the Devil ever keep it up! Deception and loss were involved, making it hugely painful. So what did I do? Finally by an act of my will I said, "*I forgive them*" and "God, forgive me." It helped the pain some, but again the replays came back. I repeated this process a number of times, and time heals all wounds, right? Then I began praying for salvation and blessings on their lives, and that brought the most healing. Now when the thoughts come back, I dismiss them as blessings in disguise since I went on to better things.

It is amazing what a great promise book the Bible is! It should be and is on bestsellers lists worldwide. There is a saying that goes, "Every promise in the book is mine, every chapter, every verse, and every line." How wonderful that is, but unless we find them, know them, and use them, we're not helped. That's where a good concordance in your Bible is helpful. Promise books of Scripture are wonderful tools because they are typically arranged in alphabetical order, making it simple to find specifically the promises you need, whether it is healing, finances, how great God's love is for you, or forgiveness. God forgives you and also enables you to forgive others. I believe every Christian would greatly benefit from having a good promise book. Book and Bible shops carry them. They can greatly help you to better relate to God, His Word, and other people and yourself.

Notes: How will you relate?

_____

_____

_____

_____

_____

_____

_____

13
Self-Relationship

How do you relate to yourself? Oh the many shades of self-relationships. They can range from loathing and self-hate to grandiosity and overblown pride. The same person may experience both at various times. In and of ourselves we can be helpless in controlling these extremes. So how should we relate to ourselves?

First and foremost it's crucial to establish our relationship with our God through Jesus Christ! He said, "No one comes to the Father but through me" (John 14:6). Once we have done that by a simple but sincere asking him to come into our heart and life and to forgive all our sin and cleanse us of all unrighteousness, we are now beginning the most important relationship in any human being's life. To say it is life changing is a bit of an understatement because it is also for you eternity changing! You are now guaranteed the most amazing and wonderful "forever and ever" in heaven with the Lord God and all your loved ones who also had a personal relationship with Jesus Christ. That is a Bible promise. "At the moment you draw your last breath that happens" (2 Corinthians 5:8). The apostle Paul said, "To be absent from the body is to be present with the Lord" for every believer. Jesus said to the thief on the cross who repented, "Today you will be with me in paradise" (Luke 23:43). It doesn't get any plainer than that! Life changing it is!

The first step is to receive and accept the freeing of guilt and shame in your life as it is now removed and gone by the Lord's forgiveness. If you have hurt and wronged someone, you do need to apologize, and if you have stolen something, you need to return it or make restitution by replacing it. The Lord will help you to do the right thing. The peace and joy to your soul and self-esteem will be so great and well worth the pain or embarrassment it may temporarily give you. The peace lasts forever. The next step is to forgive yourself and stop self-condemnation. This may not be easy if you have been doing this for a long time. But when the Lord forgives you, he forgets all those past sins and then removes them, and it is as if they are buried in the deepest sea. Forgive yourself, and stop beating up on yourself for the past. It's over and can't be undone, so now move forward into your new life. Asking the Lord for his leading and guidance will help keep you on the right path.

Reading his Word and searching out that joyous, Spirit-led church family will become the delight of your life. God's Word says, "Faith comes by hearing and hearing the word of God" (Romans 10:19). It also says, "Forsake not the gathering of yourselves together as the manner of some is" (Hebrews 10:25). So church is important in every believer's life. There you find faith, fellowship, worship, help, good friends, and most importantly, being in God's presence. There is so much joy in healing for spirit, mind, and body. Also choose wisely with prayer and God's leading because finding the right church is one of the most important choices you'll make! Visit a few services unti)l you know it's the place God wants you to be. I have been in Word- and faith-based churches now about thirty-five years and absolutely love it! Don't be put off because people clap or raise their hands. The Bible also says, "Make a joyful noise unto the Lord" (Psalms 66:1).

For many years my husband and I went through serious health challenges. Both of us had heart attacks, he had cancer and knee replacements, and I had glaucoma and diabetes. You can see that after raising, feeding, clothing, and educating three sons and three daughters, life didn't become a bed of roses. But God, our church, and our faith brought us through these bumpy rides. They were always there, and Pastor Ron's visits and Wednesday and Sunday messages were and still are a gift! Our children and grandchildren are also gifts and blessing of great price. Also my sisters and brother are such blessings. Then my in-law children, nieces, and nephews all add color and richness and joy to life.

Happiness is a decision! The secret to that fact is your self-talk, which governs what you also say out loud. That also governs what comes into your life. What you say is what you get. The Bible says, "Out of the heart the mouth speaketh" (Mathew 12:34). The devil loves nothing more than doubt and unbelief and negative speech! That gives him the right to go about and fulfill all those things you expect and said will happen. Remember God's Word says, "The devil goes about as a roaring lion seeking whom he may destroy" (1 Peter 5:8). The exact opposite of that is knowing the promises for believers in God's Word and claiming them and speaking them. That takes precedence and allows God to operate and bring about what his Word promises. This shows us the importance of reading and studying and hearing God's Word.

Remember, every promise in the book in mine. So let's take a closer look at our self-talk. What we say out loud can put the wheels in motion for either good or evil in our lives. When you are with a group of people, it is amazing the words you may hear. We have all been guilty of really negative statements. In the church I attend, we taught God's Word is true, and he means what he says. We especially live under the New Testament covenant and promises. It is filled with how much our Father God loves us and how he wants to prosper us to be in good health.

Oh how the Lord protects our going out and coming in. He wants to give his godly children the desires of our hearts. Our means to receiving these blessings is believing, asking, and receiving in faith. It goes without saying we need to familiarize ourselves with what his Word says we have. Then speak the Word to God and ourselves in every situation and need as they arise.

On the other side of the coin, what we hear a lot of can and does wreak havoc in the speakers' lives. For instance we've all heard when colds or flus are going around someone will say, "I always get it." Well you can be pretty certain that person will. The devil doesn't miss those opportunities. What we say is what we get. Be very careful what negative statements you make. They can very well happen in your life. People have brought all kinds of tragedies and disasters into their lives by voicing their fears and expectations that they will happen. They have opened the door for that very thing to happen.

Remember the Bible says in John 10:10, "The thief comes not but to steal, kill and destroy. I come that they might have life and live more abundantly." Those are Jesus' words, and that is why it's so important for every believer, new and old, to know what God's Word says so you can claim it and apply it to you personally. Never lose sight of the fact that the devil is the killer and destroyer. There is also warning in God's Word that says, "My people are destroyed by lack of knowledge" (Hosea 4:6). We aren't able to claim, use, or stand on God's promises if we don't know what they are! That's where a good promise book, along with your Bible, can dramatically change your life! But only reading them and not changing your thoughts and speech won't help you at all. You need to exercise faith and then begin to speak it out and act as though it's yours and you will have it as God's Word also says Mark 11:23-24.

Notes: How will you relate?

_____

_____

_____

_____

_____

_____

_____

14
Self-Talk

If you act in faith, you will have what you say, bearing out the power in our words. Your self-talk determines what you will say and do. That's why it is crucial to feed your mind and heart and spirit on God's Word. You can't grow and prosper on a starvation diet. Begin to consciously speak the Word into situations and believe you have the outcome in Jesus' name. Do not utter words of doubt and unbelief, for you will simply cancel your faith and Satan will jump in and bring about exactly the opposite of what you prayed for.

That's what a bit of negative confession will do. It opens the door a bit and the devil takes over. That's why the Bible speaks about how a double-minded man ought not to expect his prayers to be heard or answered. We are to walk by faith not by sight, calling those things that are not as though they are, and then we receive them. That is faith.

That principle also works for the reverse. What we

believe and say is what we get. For instance in winter if you say, "Someday I'll have an accident on black ice," count on the devil trying to make it happen. I have been involved in both situations. The first time I really rear-ended a little Volkswagen whose turning signal light was covered with mud. The second time I was coming from a Woman's Aglow meeting and had learned some things. I was driving alone, just rejoicing in the Spirit. Well in Minnesota in early spring, the streets can become glazed like a skating rink. At an intersection I hit some ice and seemed like I was flying toward the passenger's door of the car coming in front of me. I screamed, "Lord, help me," and just inches from impact, my guardian angels turned my car a full forty-five-degree angle right, and no impact occurred! It was miraculous! In the Psalms it says, "I will give my angels charge over thee" (Psalms 91:11), and he did. Promises and prayer make all the difference. They actually save our lives. I'm still travelling to speak and sing for Christian clubs in several states, and what a comfort to know I have His protection with all the craziness on the highways these days!

God is an ever-present help in times of trouble. You can literally change your life by changing your self-talk and what you say! If you tend to be a negative person and a chronic complainer, it won't be easy to change, but it can be done. Begin by studying all that God promises His children. Confess and ask forgiveness for your past doubt and unbelief, and ask for his help and guidance toward faith and praise. You can become the happiest and most fulfilled person. Your friends will want to know what you've got and how to get it. What a perfect way to share

your secret. When troubles come, you are now prepared
to handle them with the Lord!

Notes: How will you relate?

_____

_____

_____

_____

_____

_____

_____

15
God's Promises

Just to pique your curiosity, I'm going to help you out a little with some of the great promises the Lord had given to his children (you and me) who have made him the Lord of our lives. Here's a few:

1. Provision: This is really important, isn't it? "My God shall supply all your needs according to his riches in glory by Christ Jesus" (Phil. 4:19). "The Lord is my shepherd, I shall not want" (Ps. 23:4). There are so many more for you to discover.

2. Health and healing: God's Word has much to say about our heavenly Father's desire for his children to live in divine health. Even we earthly parents wish that for our children. However, we humans have sin, self, and the devil to deal with. Our words can bring all manner of sickness and disease, even death upon up by careless talk, as well as our lifestyle choices of food and beverages. The devil uses all of the above for destruction and death. But there is help and hope in God's Word to all who put their trust and faith in Him. Here are a few verses to stand on: Psalm 103:3–4 says, "Who forgives all your iniquities (sin) and heals all your diseases. Who redeems your life from destruction, who crowns you with loving kindness and tender mercies?" You should read the rest of Psalm 103. It is filled with nuggets of pure gold. Also see 1 Peter 2:24, where it says, "He bore our sins in his own body on the tree so now we should live righteously, and by his stripes we were healed." So there is hope and healing based on God's Word. Countless thousands of people have testified to miraculous healing from all kinds of sickness, deadly diseases, and accidents. You can find so many Scriptures in both the Old and New Testaments with a good Bible concordance or promise book on health or healing.

3. Finances: Yes, the Bible has a lot to say on both giving and receiving. Both are of vital interest to most Christians. The Bible does not say money is the root of all evil. It does say the love of money is the root of all evil. That is a big difference! The Lord gives his children the ability to get wealth. There are many very wealthy Christians who use their wealth according to God's principles of giving and receiving. In 3 John 2 it says, "Beloved

I wish above all things thou mayest prosper and be in health even as your soul prospers." Proverbs 13:22 says, "A good man leaves an inheritance to his children's children and the wealth of the sinner is laid up for the just [righteous]." So you see, God desires both health and prosperity for his children. This is where knowledge of God's work and belief and faith come into play. God's Word also says, "My people perish for lack of knowledge" (Proverbs 4:7). Every Christian, new or mature, young or old, needs wisdom, which can only come from feasting on the gourmet food at God's banqueting table! You can't stand on the promises if you don't know what they are. Any question you might have can be answered in God's holy Word if you use the helps to find them. Now you too can relate to His Word. Make faith-based positive statements and confessions of receiving what you pray for! Don't ever cancel them out by saying negative, doubtful words and statements! The devil will make sure they are the ones that happen so he can win and fill you with doubt and unbelief.

4. Marriage: Wow! That institution surely has taken some nasty hits and been turned upside down in a few states, including recently my state of Minnesota. I'm not proud of that. In November 2012, I wrote a letter that was printed on the opinion page of our newspaper stating the un-equivocal sanctity of marriage in both the Old and New Testament. Sodom and Gomorrah were incinerated in the Old Testament for homosexual and sexual depravity. That's where the word *sodomy* comes from. In the New Testament in Romans 1:26–28 God gave them over to a reprobate mind for their homosexual activates, both men and women. The Bible also says, "A man shall leave father and mother and cleave unto his wife and the two shall become one flesh" (Genesis 2:24). That's about as clear as it can get! That's female and singular. The Bible gives no leeway for argument or substitution. The Lord is able to change and heal anyone whose desires have gone in the wrong direction if he or she truly wants to be healed. Prayer and counseling can and have brought that about for many people. They now enjoy a normal marriage and family. God is able!

5. Giving, tithes, and offerings: That's a touchy subject for some Christians. Again God's Word gives pretty clear guidance on this subject. So that's the authority for people who love and desire to please the Lord align themselves with. First of all the Word is full of how much God loves us and has freely given us all things, including our very lives and existence. He said, "I knew you before you were assembled in your mother's womb" (Jeremiah 1:5). He continues to lavish his love and blessings on his children daily as we walk in faith and expectation and thankfulness. The Word is filled with promises of this provision. It also is very clear on what we, his children, are called to do. We can't expect to only be receivers and takers of God's goodness! We are also to be generous givers. One of his great all-encompassing promises is found in Philippians 4:19: "My God shall supply all my needs according to his riches in glory by Christ Jesus."

How wonderful is that? Now let's look at what our part is to fulfill. Tithing is strongly adhered to throughout the Old Testament. Leviticus 27:30 is just one of many references: "And the entire tithe [10 percent] of the land whether of the seed of the lord or the fruit of the tree is the Lords; it is holy unto the Lord." In Malachi 3:8 it says, "Will a man rob god? And yet you have robbed me in tithes and offerings." In verse 10 it says, "Bring ye all the tithes into my house and prove me now says the Lord that I will open the windows of heaven and pour you out a blessing that there shall not be room enough to receive it." Verses 11 and 12 are filled with great promises. Now let's see what the New Testament has to say about tithing and giving. Jesus said in Luke 6:38, "Give and it shall be given unto you, good measure pressed down, shaken together and running over shall men give unto your bosom. For with the same measure that you give, it shall be measured to you again." In 2 Corinthians 9:6–7 it says, "But this I say, He which serves sparingly shall also reap sparingly and he who sows bountifully shall also reap bountifully. Every man as he purposes in his hear, not grudgingly for God loves a cheerful giver." In Mathew 7:7 Jesus said, "Ask and it shall be given you, seek and you will find, knock, and it shall be opened unto you, for every one that asks, receives and he that seeks finds and he that knocks, it shall be opened." We clearly see the principles set forth on the abundant life. When it comes to giving and receiving, how do you relate?

6. Neighbors: This is such a friendly sounding word. Unfortunately there are people who hate their neighbors for reasons large or small. For followers of Christ, that's not acceptable. In Leviticus 19:18 God tells his people, "Love your neighbor as you love yourself." In Mark 12:30–31 Jesus said, "The first commandment is love the Lord with all your heart, soul and mind. You shall love your neighbor as yourself. There is no other commandment greater than these!" Wow, that doesn't leave much room for questions, does it? Then who is our neighbor? On hearing these words from Jesus in Luke10 a certain lawyer, trying to justify himself, stood up in verse 29 said, "Who is my neighbor? Jesus answered with the parable in the next many verses of the Good Samaritan. He told how a man traveling to Jericho fell among thieves, who stripped and beat him and left him half dead. Both a priest and then a Levite saw him and passed on the other side. Then a Samaritan came along and saw him and had compassion on him. He poured oil and wine on his wounds, bound them up, and then put him on his beast and brought him to an inn and cared for him all night. The next day he paid for him to be cared for until he returned, and then he would pay the rest of the bill. In Luke 10:36 Jesus said to the lawyer, "Which of these three men was the neighbor of the man who fell among thieves?" The lawyer answered, "The one who showed mercy to the man." Then Jesus said to him, "Go and do thou likewise." Think of the many levels of care of the Good Samaritan. It was inconvenient; he sacrificed his time, his own comfort, his supplies, and money out of his pocket for the man's care. What an example for us to live up to!

Granted some neighbors are easier to love than others. How should one handle a neighbor who does ongoing, irritating things? As a follower of the Lord, first pray for his help and guidance as to how to approach them. Then with a civil attitude and tone of voice, facial expression, and body language, go and speak to them. Tell them how it affects you and how you feel. Let them know that you would appreciate it if they would change or stop doing it. A smile and kindly attitude will go further than threats. If you are on the receiving end from a neighbor for something you do, carefully examine his or her complaint. If it's legitimate, apologize and change, and don't do it anymore. As a Christian you need to be a good example of testimony to bring glory to the Lord's name. So how do you relate to your neighbor?

Notes: How will you relate?

_____

_____

_____

_____

_____

_____

_____

16
Changing Circumstances

Change brings excitement to some and dread to others. It depends on how large or dramatic the change is going to be. Many experience real anxiousness. We tend to like and feel comfortable in our routines, but often change is necessary. Most of us are very aware that we could benefit if we made some changes here and there. Many people make New Year's resolutions with good intentions but find after a short time they're not doing very well.

So what's the problem? Well there's a saying that pretty well sums it up: "The definition of insanity is doing the same thing over and over and expecting different results!" Obviously we need to put some serious thought into the changes we want to make. If we are experiencing fear and anxiety, we need to pray for that to be overcome and then seek guidance on how to proceed. People look

73

at risk, and they weigh cost to benefits. How far out of my comfort will I have to go? What is the cost in time, money, and convenience? Sometimes plain old laziness plays a part. But if we know in our hearts and our spirits that God wants us to change, then if we want his blessing and we want to move forward, we will spend some serious time in his Word and prayer.

There is often a tendency to procrastinate, which is actually disobedience. We're all different and have various reasons why change can seem different, and usually there's an element of risk. "What if I don't succeed, don't like it, and can't keep it up?" The devil knows our weak spots and uses every fiery dart in his arsenal to defeat us. But we have the greater one, and he can give us the courage to win! In Romans 12:2 it says, "And be not conformed to this world but be transformed [changed] by the renewing of your mind that you may prove what is that good and acceptable and perfect will of God!"

Oh my, I'm home again! I just got home from thirteen days of travel to four countries in Europe: England (London), France (Paris), Switzerland, and Italy. I traveled with my youngest daughter. I have been on this tour before with my husband years ago, but it was a first time with one of my children. And we had a wonderful time! But you'd better be ready for change! Every day was different! Scenery, food, beds, and tour guide. Also a fast pace and late to bed and early to rise and down to a big breakfast for grace and patience with the loud people on the bus and the many little things that can arise daily when you are on a completely new routine. Actually it's a good experience to get you out of your comfort zone and put into practice some of those Christian virtues you are working on!

Change at any age isn't easy for most of us. But it's necessary in life because nothing stays the same very long. Change takes place all around us. It's easy to get comfortable and set in our ways. It's another thing when we decide to make change. Even then it can be difficult, but so many things can change out of our control and sometimes so quickly. That's when the rubber hits the road on how we handle it.

Sometimes they can be a crushing blow! They are the hardest, so what do we do? Well, first of all don't panic; turn to our Comforter, our heavenly Father. He is always there with open arms! He is all wise, all knowing, and can give us peace in the middle of the storm! Ask him to guide and lead and give you answers. The Holy Spirit can do all of the above if we ask and receive it. The Holy Spirit leads us into all truth. He will give us patience and understanding and help us do what we need to do.

You might ask, "How do I access or be in a position to have the Holy Spirit help me?" First of all you need to be a born-again believer in Jesus Christ and have a personal relationship with him. Then we must do as in the second chapter of Acts, where the believers were all gathered together. Jesus ascended into heaven and sent the Holy Spirit, and they were all filled and began to speak in other languages. This is called the day of Pentecost. Years later some of the disciples went to speak to the Christians in Samaria that Philip in Acts 8:8–12 had preached to and baptized, and they all received the Holy Spirit by the laying on of hands.

I was born and baptized Lutheran and went to church and one year of Lutheran high school out of the four years. But at that time they didn't teach about the infilling of the Holy Spirit. Years later during the renewal of the baptism of the Holy Spirit nationwide, some branches of the Lutheran churches had huge conference on the Holy Spirit in Minneapolis and were teaching on correctly and fully as the Bible does.

However one doesn't have to be at a conference or even have the laying on of hands. I was awakened at three in the morning (my sister Phyllis had given me a couple of books about it), and the Spirit's presence was so powerful I just asked him to come in and fill me, and he did. It changed my life forever! The Bible says if we ask for the infilling of the Holy Spirit, he will come in and fill us, and we will practice the gifts of the Holy Spirit as mentioned in the last verses in the book of Mark and also Acts. So if you are a born–again believer in Jesus Christ, all you need to do is ask and receive. It's perhaps better if you are in a church where they practice the laying on of hands and have some helpful literature. But it's best to find an alive, friendly Pentecostal church where they teach and practice this very important part of the Bible. It will make your walk with the Lord so joyful and intimate, and you can even imagine the difference it makes! I was a Christian for years before receiving the infilling (baptism) of the Holy Spirit, and there's no comparison. The Assemblies of God is one denomination that practices it.

Change—there's that word again, but oh how we need it in our country and our homes and schools. Revival and renewal are desperately needed to turn our country around. It is the heart cry and prayer of godly people all across our land. The statistics of church attendance among the middle and younger generation are quite shocking. Parents and schools are to blame. They keep lowering the age of sex education to really young children. Of course our anti-God people try hard to keep God and religion out of our schools! Parents need to be vigilant about what goes on in their schools and textbook content! We need to pray for our schools and good teachers and not passively stand by if you know there are teachers actively pushing a liberal, anti-God agenda to your children. You certainly have a right and duty to speak to school boards and teachers. Check out their textbooks. It's your tax dollars that pay their salaries. When it comes to your kids' schools, how do you relate?

When it comes to change, many of us could really improve our lives if we with God's help would get a grip on that unruly member, our tongue. That's what the Bible calls it. It's full of evil and deadly poison. It's difficult to hear, but in today's world it's necessary! We will see what it says about it in James 3. Almost the entire chapter of James is filled with metaphors of huge things that can controlled with really small appliances, such as a rudder on a huge ship, a bridle in a horse's mouth, and wild, large animals that can be trained and tamed. But the tongue is a small and unruly member and like a spark can set a whole forest on fire, so can the tongue start all manners of fires! James goes on to say it is a restless evil full of deadly poison. A wise person should read and study James 3. The last verse speaks of two kinds of wisdom. Do a bit reading, to get the one that comes down from heaven.

Our world is so full of the other kind that we need all the help the Word and the Lord can give us. Having the joy of the Lord makes us a different kind of person. How do you and your tongue relate?

Words are truly amazing things! They are prolific products! You can use them to do amazing things in your life! They are strong, and they are powerful. You can make them work for you or against you. I must admit I am fascinated by them. Now faith is a powerful word. Hebrews 11:1 says, "Now faith is the substance [raw material] of things hoped for, the evidence of things not seen." Then Romans 10:17 says, "So then faith comes by hearing and hearing the word of God." So the combination of the Word of God and faith can and has created miracles. So in the life of a Christian, it is an essential and integral part! Without faith it is impossible to please God, the Bible says. It then is incumbent on us to find all the wonderful things God has promised to us, his children. A Bible in today's English with a concordance and a good Scripture promise book are godsends.

What an adventure learning all God wants to bless you with! Your faith and your words will delight the Lord and make them a reality in your life. As a believer God has given you the same measure of faith He gives to every believer. It is yours to nourish and grow by reading, hearing, and exercising it. Put yourself in a vibrant Bible- and faith-teaching church. Then make your words line up exactly with what the Bible says you have. Then by faith you shall receive it.

The Lord wants to bless you; he's your heavenly Father. So don't let doubt or negative words cancel what

He wants to give you. The Bible says a double-minded person doesn't receive because that is doubt and unbelief. Make your confession, "Your Word says it, I believe it, that settles it, and I receive it. Thank you, Lord." Find Scriptures that specifically cover your need. Whether it's financial, health and healing, a job, whatever your need, you can find it in your Bible concordance, Bible dictionary, or promise book. There is a verse in the Bible that says, "My God shall supply all my needs according to His riches in glory by Christ Jesus" (Philippians 4:19). So if you have a real need, you have permission and in fact a right to pray for it and believe and expect the Lord to answer. That's his promise. It doesn't say he will supply all greed or selfishness, however. Also we are to be givers as well as receivers.

It is vital for you to understand how important your self-talk is. That determines what you believe, and that becomes your spoken word. What you speak brings that reality into your life. If people would grasp that truth, they could avoid all kinds of trouble and woe! Yes even tragedy. There is a ton of truth in the saying, "What you say is what you get!" Learning that has really changed my life. I try very hard not to make negative statements that open the door for the devil to make them a reality in my life.

Remember, the Bible tells us he goes about as a roaring lion seeking whom he (and his demons) may destroy. God's Word encourages us to use positive, healthy, power-filled speech. Our loving heavenly Father wants only good things for his children. He never, ever puts sickness or disease on anyone. He is never the one to cause tragedy or accident! The Bible is full of the blessings and protection He will provide for us. Again, we can't stand on the promises if we don't know what they are! Hosea 4:6 says, "My people are destroyed by lack of knowledge." That's the reason people of God experience every kind of life's problems: sickness, accidents, and tragedies. We need to feast on God's Word to know the depth of His love, provision, protection, divine health, mental health, and joy. He desires this for us and more!

The power of the tongue and words are in many Bible verses, and here are just a few of them. Proverbs 18:20–21 says, "A man's belly shall be satisfied with the fruit of his mouth and with the increase of his lips shall he be filled. Death and life are in the power of the tongue and they that love it shall eat the fruit thereof." That really does show us the power of words! We can create all manner of blessings in our lives by the words we use. Thoughtless, careless, and negative words bring just the opposite. It takes mindful practice.

The Psalms and Proverbs are a goldmine of wisdom, and so much of them are beautiful reading. Again it's so good to accentuate the positive, eliminate the negative, latch on to the affirmative, don't mess with the halfway stuff in-between. Living by God's promises will change your life so much! Use them to encourage others, mend relationships, and make new friends. Use words of praise and thanksgiving when you're talking to the Lord. Use your self-talk to encourage yourself, reminding yourself you are beloved by God. You can't imagine how much it makes you want to love and serve him with all your heart!

I believe it is so important it bears repeating, where

the Bible says, "My people perish because of a lack of knowledge." It also says, "Faith comes by hearing the word of God" (Rom. 10:17). It is essential to study and meditate on God's Word ad also to hear it preached and taught by qualified pastors and Bible study leaders. You just can't do better for yourself than to surround yourself with these and other believers in a good church. They actually do become your extended family. What a wonderful support system! Pray and seek, and you will find such a church, and attending it will be a joy you will look forward to. It will build your faith, and you will grow in knowledge and truth, which is so important in our faith walk in this difficult world.

If you find yourself in a rather dead and boring church, you need to do some checking and visiting to other churches so the Lord can direct you to the right one! Don't be surprised if it isn't the denomination of your parents, or one you have been attending infrequently. What is important is if it is really alive and teaching and preaching the Word boldly and with real love for God and each other. Visit a few, and trust the Lord to lead you to the right one where he wants you to be. Pray and listen to His leading. Believe me, the effort will be well worth it. You can't imagine the blessings of being in a vibrant church where the pastors and people truly love and serve God and each other!

I have now been in my church going on twenty-five years and am so happy to be here. There is a sad commentary on church hopping by too many of today's churchgoers. They find a church and stay, become involved and active for a period of time, and then disappear. Some make that a pattern and are always looking for something new and seem easily bored. If they truly sought God's guidance while they were looking, in all likelihood they would have found a true home church where they would want to stay. Having a disagreement with the pastor or other members is not a good reason to leave. These are opportunities to practice forgiveness and brotherly love.

If you are in a good, God-loving church, step out of your comfort zone and offer your help and services. You will find you are blessed and a blessing. A church has so many areas for which they can use your gifts and talents. In all endeavors, you are serving God and man. All churches have a variety of people, so you will probably have to practice a variety of Christian virtues. That's a good thing that helps you grow and mature in God's family. It makes life interesting.

We recently had a large influx of people from a couple different countries. Wow! Talk about a need to change and be flexible in our congregation! We had been praying for an increase in membership, but we had not envisioned people so different from ourselves! There are so many different things they need: language teaching, transportation, finding housing and work. Many speak English fairly well, and the oldest are learning. One Sunday a month we use a young man along with Pastor Ron to translate the sermon. It works well and is a good learning experience for all of us. We feel they are a blessing to all of us at every age. It certainly presents us with many opportunities to show Christ's love. They seem to like us and are comfortable being part of our church family. Most of them had embraced Christianity and were persecuted in their country for that reason. We count them as blessings and present an opportunity to grow in grace and love.

It just seemed to happen out of the blue to us, but it was part of God's plan to bless all of us. One Sunday our church seemed to overflow with carloads of strangers. It was really quite amazing to see! They have very different names, their women wear very colorful clothing, we experience different foods at our love feasts, and after many months they are still with us. God works in mysterious ways His wonders to perform! I think we are doing a good job embracing these precious people into our church. How would you relate?

My closing thoughts and prayers deeply desire that you find help, hope, and answers to the many situations that frequently occur in virtually any relationship. God has the answers. Seek and you will find them. God bless!

Notes: How will you relate?

_____

_____

_____

_____

_____

_____

_____

Life: How Do You Relate

Life's journey begins as a tiny little tot—
At its conception, scarcely more than a teeny, tiny dot.
God's amazing miracle that leads to birth
Brought us Beethoven and Einstein
and, yes, Jesus to earth.

In the beginning, God created Adam and Eve.
We all know he already had a lot up his sleeve.
Our first parents failed and made a mess for us;
Now life's often a struggle as we fume and fuss.

The stages of life that we all go through
Involve learning, study, and experiences old and new.
How we choose to involve, respond, and relate
Determines so much of our lives,
work, and love, not fate.

So many paths invite us to choose.
Remember, with God's help, we can win and not lose
As we move through the stages that we will in life.
With God as your tour guide, have joy and less strife.

Each stage has its benefits, large and small.
Childhood, student, and siblings come to almost all.
Love, peace, and prosperity are most people's choice.
The closer you walk with the Lord,
the more you will rejoice.

To sum up our help in a few brief lines,
The go-to person, Jesus Christ, radiantly shines.
He's the supreme teacher, helper, and healer to all.
Go to Him; no situation or problem
is too large or small.
He loves you so deeply. He's awaiting your call.
God loves you, and so do I.

Written by Eloise Windahl-Deihl

CPSIA information can be obtained at www.ICGtesting.com
Printed in the USA
LVOW12s0802200814

399914LV00001B/1/P

9 781489 702203